So . . . What Happens to the PACKAGE?

So . . . What Happens to the PACKAGE?

Robert E. Daley

The Larry Czerwonka Company, LLC
Hilo, Hawai‘i

First Edition — August 2014

Published by: The Larry Czerwonka Company
http://thelarryczerwonkacompany.com

Printed in the United States of America

ISBN: 0692263373
ISBN-13: 978-0692263372

BOOKS BY ROBERT E. DALEY

The Enhancement Series

#1 Book of Ecclesiastes
#2 Book of Daniel
#3 Book of Romans
#4 Book of Galatians
#5 Book of Hebrews

The Deeper Things of God Series

#1 The Personage of God
#2 The Personage of Man
#3 The Personage of Christ

Introduction

This is a love letter, and a story about Human Beings. A story about every Human Being that has ever come into existence. A story about **YOU** and **ME**. A story about Truth and Reality. A story about Time and Eternity. A story about Life and Death. So, it is this author's prayer that the information presented, will not be frivolously laughed at, or ignored, nor dealt with in a cavalier manner by **YOU**, the one who is reading this right now. And because of the sensitivity of the subject, we will not be *beating around the bush*, or going down the emotional corridor of *Aww . . . poor thing.*

Sadly, there are certain things that Human Beings do not take very seriously, until it is far too late. And indeed, this story does have a *point of no return.*

This author is wide open, to whosoever may be able to present a solid case showing how there is no validity in this story. I challenge **YOU** to do so. Otherwise . . . give some serious, sober, time of thought, to this simplistic tale, which relays a very real truth. And then know

that from the moment **YOU** have finished reading this short story there will no longer be any
acceptable excuses for your lack of understanding as to how things actually work. For then as
YOU stand before the Living God of all creation, your denial, ignorance, or feigned declara-
tions, that things do not really work that way,
and the outcome should be different will fall
upon deaf ears . . . well aware that you now
know better.

Enjoy this story, consider what is said, and
then please act upon the option that is given unto
YOU at the conclusion of this work.

Maranatha!

The Prelude

From as far back in time as this author can remember, whenever a brand new Human baby was birthed onto this planet, references have been made, by other Human Beings, as to how precious the new little one was; or of the professed innocence that was declared concerning this new life; or what a cute *bundle* of joy was smiling from within the warm receiving blanket.

For the sake of our story, we will draw from the terminology of the Human *bundle*, and henceforth refer to that specific *bundle* that we will be talking about, which includes **YOU**, as the **Package**.

* * *

Now, the subject of physical DEATH is quite real. It is not a very popular subject, but that does not mean that physical DEATH is not real. Contact a dear friend, who has physically died recently, and ask them if DEATH is something that is real. Contact departed grandpa, or grandma, or auntie, or nephew, or a neighbor, or a movie star, or a famous politician, or a leader of a nation, or a king, and ask them if physical DEATH is something that is truly real, or not.

And if **YOU** are not able to personally contact them, and substantiate concerning their own unique testimony, as to whether or not physical DEATH is something real, then please, let us not attempt to politically correct ourselves into deception, concerning this issue.

Are you anxious, or afraid, or personally upset yet? Has a fear of the unknown darkness blatantly attacked you, concerning what we are talking about? Have you decided, even before we get to our simple Story, that these issues are just too sensitive and scary, because they might challenge the misconceptions, misnomers, lies, myths, and other ideas that you have come to *believe* in, and rely on, during your short tenure on this planet? Are **YOU** able to sum up enough courage to read through this harmless little booklet . . . or are **YOU** finished?

* * *

Now . . . the Devil is another subject that is quite real. He does not necessarily like the spotlight to be turned upon him, and expose him for who he really is, but that does not mean that he does not exist, and is not real. And what **YOU** may personally *believe,* concerning the Devil, has nothing to do with it whatsoever.

You may *believe* as other men have in the past that the moon is made out of green cheese, or that aliens built the pyramids, or that the Theory of Evolution is based upon valid science . . . but the moon and the pyramids and creation realities do not care one whit what **YOU** *believe.*

Contact someone credible who knows about spiritual truths. Contact someone who has spent much more time and energy than **YOU** have, on subjects of an invisible nature, and ask them what they know about the subject of the Devil or Creation.

Or maybe . . . there really is no absolute truth at all. Maybe there is nothing that is the baseline; nothing that is foundational. Maybe the Devil really is a figment of someone's imagination. Maybe the Devil and his fallen angels and the other holy angels and God Himself are not real, and there is nothing of a definite certainty, except the indisputable issue of physical DEATH.

Is that the position that **YOU** would prefer? Do **YOU** really want to base your entire existence on shifting sand?

* * *

Rest assured that a specific location within the bowels of this planet Earth, called HELL, is quite real. It is a subject of controversy to be sure. Many times the same Human Beings that *believe* in Evolution, also choose to *believe* that HELL is not a real place, but rather is figurative. After all, if the *God* that we hear so much about is really a God of love, then why would a heinous complex like a fiery, tormenting HELL be needed?

Don't all Human Beings, when the specter of physical DEATH arrives, simply whisk off into heaven (if it too really does exist)? Isn't the solace of mental and emotional tranquility available, concerning the *afterlife* when the ugliness of DEATH's finality, rears its sin-scarred head? How about *soul-sleep* . . . should we choose that option? Or maybe, if we have been good enough, we will find that we have earned our wings, and shall now become some holy angel, and shall try to help others in need.

Finally, God, The Creator, is another subject that is quite real. And the God of incalculable love, who gave all He had in order to specifically obtain **YOU**, is not trying to hide or make Himself scarce. He is right out in the open, and He wants all Human Beings to know about Him, and to know what He has done. In spite of the spiritual innuendos, outright lies, doctrinal falsehoods, and projected deceptions, He has not changed, nor altered the magnificent plan that He has put forth for all who would be willing to listen to Him. Will **YOU** be willing to listen?

Do **YOU** know God personally . . . or do you only know about God? Can **YOU** give this author a bevy of collected information, that years of table-talk, or childhood remembrances, or promoted falsehood, have formulated? Or, can **YOU** personally introduce this author to the Living Lord of Hosts, just like **YOU** would introduce him to one of your relatives, or good friends?

The Story that follows is designed to present a simple illustration of spiritual realities. Our prayer is that spiritual insight may be granted by the Holy Spirit of Truth Himself, to every reader of this work, that none should perish but that all would make a wise decision for life evermore, including **YOU**.

A Cadre of Spiritual Realities

#1. The God that we speak of in this work, who is quite real, originally created this Universe that we now live in and currently observe.

#2. Other moral creatures were created before Human Beings were, and all of those moral creatures rebelled against the God of Love, and received righteousness judgment for their actions.

#3. Among those who rebelled, there was a holy angel who carried great anointing and authority.

#4. As part of his personal judgment, he fell from grace, was demoted, and had his name changed to Satan, or the Devil, to reflect his new sin-defiled nature.

#5. He was allowed to remain at liberty (for legal reasons) and was on the scene when God The Creator, purposed to bring forth an unprecedented moral creature into existence, called the Human Being. That's **YOU**!

#6. The Human Being was originally created *in* God's image, and *after* God's likeness, and was given power and authority over all that God had created.

#7. God's focused purpose for the Human Being was that he would become an actual *child* of God, and an actual member of His household.

#8. God set His new creation into a testing-lab habitat, and issued initial instructions. In strict simplicity, eat from, and enjoy, all of the food producing vegetation, except one.

#9. If that one food producing vegetation is eaten from, then the very real condition of DEATH will occur. First . . . Spiritual, and then . . . Physical.

#10. That DEATH will affect every Human Being that comes forth into existence . . . without exception!

The Story

Adam was brand-spanking new. He had never experienced the early *bundle* condition, but that did not alter the reality that he was indeed a **Package**, under the ownership of someone.

He was an extremely smart Human Being, and a quick study, and he knew what he was supposed to do. Eve, his lovely wife, was also a **Package**, and similarly intelligent, and personally owned as well; but in their early days of time together, she had not been completely tutored by her husband, in every aspect that she should have been.

Together, they enjoyed a marvelous time with one another; exploring and hiking through the Garden, and reveling in their infusion with all of the flowers and trees, and animal life that was all around them. The fresh fruits and vegetables from the various trees and vines were delicious, but that forbiddance of the one tree in the middle of the Garden was curious.

The serpent was also quite subtle. And, his recent collusion with the Devil, and the promise of exaltation was stimulating to him. He purposed to cheerfully greet the woman, every time their paths crossed, so that at the appropriate moment his queries would not seem out of place to her.

On a given day, after a time of interacting sweet communion, the close proximity of Adam and the woman to the forbidden tree presented the opportune moment.

Casual conversation with the woman, leading to a challenge, surprised the serpent when no objection was raised by Adam. Continued verbiage and a consummating tasting of the forbidden fruit by the woman, all but closed the deal. Right before his very eyes the radiance within the woman began to diminish. And with her arm extended, fruit in hand, Adam's capitulation became realized as he too partook of the temptation, and he ushered in the DEATH sentence upon all of Humanity.

Since the unwritten law of the program from the outset was that an individual became owned by the one, to whom that person chose to obey. And, as such, the original spiritual ownership labels that were placed on the **Packages** of Adam and now the woman had to be altered. New labels had to be made to reflect that Adam and the woman now no longer spiritually belonged to God (who had originally created them for His own good pleasure) but, because of their disobedience, they became the legal, spiritual property of the Devil, and were so tagged.

Adam and the woman had failed the test they were given, and were invited to leave the Garden setting. And now, through them and their offspring, DEATH would be sown into this Earth with every thought, word, and deed. It is a grim situation indeed.

Time and infused instinct within Adam and Eve produces a new life, and the innocent *bundle* of joy that comes forth brings delight to the fledging parents. They are becoming more and more spiritually numb with the passage of time, and are working their way through the manifest natural challenges of everyday life. And the already installed ownership tag, spiritually reflects that the recently delivered **Package** (even right from the womb) belongs to the Devil. Each additional child similarly finds no difference on the label decree. And as reproduction increases the species of Human Beings on the planet Earth, every single **Package** carries the ownership tag of the Devil. And there is nothing that any Human Being can do about that.

Physical life, in those early years, was extended for the Human Being species, because of the thoroughbred origin of their stock.

The Cain and Abel incident that is told, and retold, was a sad occurrence, ultimately gendered by sin-compulsive pride. Even so, physical DEATH donned the familiar shroud of finality, and the **Package** known of as Abel was delivered into the HELL complex, and to the legal owner, whose name was on the tag.

And then, even though it took a number of years to occur on a regular basis, physical DEATH finally showed up on the scene with distressing frequency. All of the Human Beings on the planet (after a relatively short period of time) were brought to the threshold of termination.

And all of them were delivered into the HELL complex, and to the owner whose name was on the tag—namely, the Devil.

[The name tag on various Human Beings living within a certain *comfort* location in the HELL complex was changed, at a point in time, and because of certain spiritual realities. But we will not touch upon the truth of how that occurred at this point.]

Century after century saw the physical DEATH finality of Human Beings, and the **Packages** that were being regularly brought into the HELL complex began to pile up and become overwhelming.

Addendum

#1. The Spiritual DEATH of Human Beings has all of the earmarks of an incurable disease. Infectious to the absolute, and no location on the planet nor application of any external remedy will protect them.

#2. The Physical DEATH of Human Beings also has all of the earmarks of an incurable disease. Applicable to every single Human Being that has come into existence, with absolutely no remedy for anyone, and that includes **YOU**. What to do?

And here is where, worldwide, willful, ignorance and deception concerning spiritual reality, separates the sheep from the goats.

Human Beings are extremely prideful creatures. How much pride do **YOU** personally have? Is there enough pride, fear, and ignorance, within **YOU**, to send **YOU** into a Christless Eternity of fiery torment when the guardian of the river Styx comes to ferry **YOU** across the threshold of finality?

YOU are not a religious person are **YOU**? After all, religion and spiritual understanding is just for fools and cowards isn't it? And you certainly are no fool, are **YOU**? And of course, you are not a coward either . . . **YOU** can muster whatever amount of emotional courage it takes to face your last moments of physical life on this Earth, without any assistance from anyone, can't **YOU**?

However, kindly inform this author as to where **YOU** *believe* **YOU** will find yourself when on the other side of DEATH? Emotions are a real poor substitute for spiritual truth. So, please invest just a few more moments of your precious life, and read the rest of this Story.

The Story Concludes . . .

Planet-wide, the Christmas Story is known by Human Beings everywhere. The attempt, by the Devil, to convert spiritual truth into the same fairy-tale status as the Easter Bunny, the Tooth Fairy, Santa Claus, and the Great Pumpkin, has seen much success.

However, that does not alter the Truth. Spiritual reality declares that the loving Creator (God), put on a suit of flesh, became a Human Being Himself, and gave his life for the sake of others.

The DEATH, and particularly the Resurrection of Jesus Christ of Nazareth, has brought about a spiritual **Name-Tag Alteration** within the Eternal mailroom of the Universe.

Prior to the resurrection of the Lord Jesus, the name-tags of ownership of every single Human Being on this planet—which includes **YOU**—declares Satan, also known as the Devil, to be the one to whom the Human Being **Package** belongs.

And, whenever a Human Being physically dies—which includes **YOU**—the angelic mailman will faithfully deliver the **Package** to the one whose name is on the ownership tag.

Don't like that idea?—that's too bad! Don't *believe* that reality?—that's too bad! And, since **YOU** are so smart, concerning things of Eternal value, **YOU** tell this author how things really do work! The foundational source that he uses to present these truths, is the Bible, the Scriptures, the Word of God. What infallible source do **YOU** present your case from?

What is it that keeps **YOU** then from making a simple decision, and trusting in what someone else did for **YOU**? Ignorance, Pride, Stubbornness, Religion, Emotion, Stupidity? What?

When a Human Being simply surrenders to the Truth, and chooses to place his trust in the work of the Son of God, the ownership nametag is altered. And that Human Being does not even have to know how it all works . . . because it is a matter of trust. The *Belongs to the Devil* tag is removed, and the new label of, *Belongs to the Living God* replaces it. And, it is just that simple.

The angelic mailmen of the Universe will deliver every single **Package** that belongs to the Devil, into the HELL complex, where unending fiery torment, excruciating pain, and utter hopelessness will swallow up young and old alike, even if **YOU** are a really *nice* person.

Those same angelic mailmen of the Universe will also deliver every single **Package** that belongs to the Living God into the heavenly scene of peace, tranquility, harmony, and love. Where there is no pain. Where there is no tormenting fire. Where there is nothing that is heinous or unpleasant.

The Creator (God) will finally obtain that for which He gave the very best that Heaven had. He will finally have the children that He has always wanted. He will finally have the person of **YOU**! And so it will be . . . for the entire ever and ever time fulfillment.

So, what is the problem? Why are **YOU** waiting? This is not really about any religion, is it? This is about Truth and Reality. What will YOUR personal choice be? Torment or Peace? The decision is strictly YOURS. With a simple desire to not perish, and with genuine sincerity, just declare with your own lips:

Dear Lord Jesus, I am a lost sinner, but I do not want to leave this world, and find myself in the HELL complex. I have heard that you died for me, and desire to make me your very own brother or sister. Please forgive me of all of my sins, and by your Holy Spirit, make me a brand new person . . . and change my package label, so that I may live with you and our Father (God) in heaven, for ever and ever. I choose to receive you as my personal Savior, and trust you for paying off my sin indebtedness. I will turn from my sins and learn of your ways. Show me the way that I should walk. Thank you, Lord Jesus, for your unconditional Love for me. Amen.

* * *

Please remember, ONLY your pride, your personal decision, your ignorance of spiritual truth, your stubbornness, your stupidity, your resistance to reality, your political correctness, or your *I don't believe in any of this spiritual stuff*, can keep **YOU** out of heaven, and send **YOU** into HELL.

Enough said. This author does not *believe* in beating a dead horse. He is simply trying to help, because he really does Love **YOU**, with the Love of Christ Jesus.

Go ahead . . . go where **YOU** want to go!

Meet the Author

By-The-Book Ministries, Inc. began in 2001 as a teaching outreach. Rob E. Daley has been gifted by God to be able to explain biblical truths in an easy to understand manner.

Many have been blessed by his teaching style.

Rob was saved and filled with the Holy Spirit in 1978 and has been instructed by the greatest teacher of all—the Spirit of Truth Himself. Rob is an ordained minister with the Assemblies of God International Fellowship and has pastored in various churches over the past 34 years.

It is the desire of this ministry to see the body of Christ solidly taught, and grow up into the things of the Lord. Rob is available for seminars, retreats, conventions, etc.

Rob can be reached at:

thedaleys@bythebookministries.org

http://robdaleyauthor.com